When Angels Speak

Inspiration from
Touched By An Angel

Martha Williamson
Executive Producer

A FIRESIDE BOOK
PUBLISHED BY SIMON & SCHUSTER

FIRESIDE
Rockefeller Center
1230 Avenue of the Americas
New York, NY 10020

Copyright © MCMXCVII CBS Inc.
All rights reserved,
including the right of reproduction
in whole or in part in any form.

FIRESIDE and colophon are registered trademarks
of Simon & Schuster Inc.

Manufactured in the United States of America

10   9   8   7   6   5

Library of Congress Cataloging-in-Publication Data
is available.

ISBN 0-684-84356-0

❦

Acknowledgments

My parents, whose wisdom and faith are reflected in every page of this book

The men and women of CBS Television, whose courage and commitment to *Touched By An Angel* continue to touch lives around the world

Roma Downey, Della Reese, and John Dye, whose extraordinary talents make the words sing

The writers and producers of *Touched By An Angel* for their dedication and passion

ACKNOWLEDGMENTS

The Staff and Crew of *Touched By An Angel*, who are themselves an inspiration to us all

Marcie Gold, who never gives up

Sonya Dunn Hodson, who never gives up either

Ed Wilson and Bob Cook, the gentlemen of Eyemark

Ken Ross

Jeff Nemerovski

Thom Parham

Suzonne Stirling

Mary Reed

❧

Introduction

*P*eople want the words. Perhaps there will come a day when America clamors for the *Touched By An Angel* lunchbox, or the official *Touched By An Angel* chewable vitamins, or maybe the limited edition Monica, Tess, and Andrew dolls. But right now, people want the words.

The words that are spoken on *Touched By An Angel* every Sunday night seem to haunt viewers during the rest of the week, and inevitably we get requests for the words to be repeated:

"Our son died of AIDS last year and your words comforted us."

INTRODUCTION

"What you said about secrets gave me the courage to confront my mother."

"When the angel talked about God knowing who I really am, I realized I had no right to take my life."

"What did Tess say last week about forgiveness? I need to hear that again."

The words of hope spoken by angels on an unlikely television show seem to be resonating in the hearts of many, many people. That is the greatest compliment we can receive, and it is our highest honor to publish those words here.

Among them you will find possibly the boldest, certainly the most popular quote from *Touched By An Angel*: "God loves you." It is the cornerstone of the series. It is the Great Truth that is so simple a concept and so stunning a declaration that it reaches right through the television screen and echoes in every living room and in every heart. It is at once comforting and disturbing, because implicit in its message of love is a challenge. God loves you. *Now what are you going to do about it?*

I was interviewed last year by a reporter from a big-city newspaper. He asked me the usual questions about ratings and time slots and guest stars. After twenty minutes, he thanked me for my answers and I assumed the interview was over. But for the next forty minutes, the reporter went "off the record." He had watched the show that week. He had heard the words "God loves you." And throughout the week he had struggled with the rest of the message: *Now* what do I do?

Remember that reporters and television critics welcomed the first season of *Touched By An Angel* the way wolves welcome a bunny rabbit to the den. But for some reason, as this critic was discovering, it didn't feel so good anymore to rip our little show to shreds.

As I listened to the reporter open his heart, I heard him trying to make sense of

Touched By An Angel. It wasn't the kind of edgy, action-driven, dark drama that journalists love to lionize. But there was something about it . . . something . . .

"Simple," I said. "It's simple. It has to be. *God* has to be. Because God must be for everyone or He is for no one. God isn't sophisticated. God is not a college graduate—God *created* them. And everyone else in this world. God loves His children . . . God loves you."

And the reporter began to cry.

Words that are true have a life of their own. We don't have to make them up. Our job at *Touched By An Angel* is simply to repeat them in the hope that they will inspire others toward self-examination and positive change. That is the highest and best goal of television, and it is our privilege to reach for it.

Martha Williamson
Los Angeles, California
February 1997

*T*iming is everything in this business.

*T*here's a rhythm to life, sweetheart. And when we disturb it, things like this happen. What we do has eternal consequences, and you've got to have faith that whatever job you're given, it matters.

ℭↄ

*D*on't be afraid. God loves you.
So much you can't even imagine it.

*L*ove doesn't hide. It stays and fights. It goes the distance. That's why God made love so strong. So it can carry you . . . all the way home.

☙

May the road rise before you.
May your swing be straight, may
the ball fly high and far, and may
God Himself bring you home.

❧

*S*ometimes you have to stand up and fight for what you believe in. And sometimes it takes even more courage to stay put, to hold your ground and refuse to be bullied . . . It doesn't change the bully. But it can change you.

*H*oney, we all die by ourselves.
It's living all by ourselves that
hurts.

*S*ome of our best living is done through the people we leave behind.

*P*eople only carry on in the dark when they don't want you to see what they're doing.

ço

You can't spend your life sitting in a boat, staying safe. That's no life.

ભ

*S*ometimes we fear what we can't control.

*L*ove erases fear.

*W*hat you need to know about the past is that no matter what has happened, it has all worked together to bring you to this very moment. And this is the moment you can choose to make everything new. Right now.

❧

*S*trong but bitter. Some people like it that way—straight ahead, rich, and undiluted. But there's another side to an espresso kind of life . . . heartburn. That's the price you pay for all that flavor.

☙

*G*od loves you . . . because you're you. You've spent your whole life running and running, trying to catch up with something that has never been there for you. Like a deer running out of fear or thirst. But never for the joy of running. And all you've done is go farther and farther away from the precious love that's been waiting for you all the time.

ॐ

*P*eople are too busy to meet themselves anymore. Everybody's faxing and modeming and on-lining and inputting and downloading and overnighting. If you don't like it, change the channel. Press the button. "Escape/ Delete." You can send anything to anybody, anywhere in the world, in seconds. But it still takes the same time it always took to know a soul, to mend a broken heart . . . to give birth to a child. Even in a world of change, some things just don't.

*S*ometimes endings are just opportunities.

*N*o such thing as late. Destiny
picks its own time.

&

*D*estiny doesn't happen. It arrives. And when it does, you either batten down the hatches and wait till it blows over, or you swing open the gates and invite it in to supper.

છ9

*T*hat's the trouble with destiny.
You never can dress for it.

❧

*T*his is a moment of truth. And love is only part of the truth. And romance . . . well, romance doesn't have much to do with either one.

*M*aybe you need to find the beauty in being alone.

*T*his is what you call an unexpected snow. One moment the sky looks clear, and the next moment the sky is falling. And you can run inside and hide, or you can become part of it and let it change you.

When there's that much pain, you gotta ask yourself if it's really love. People hold on to each other for lots of reasons they can't understand, and they call it love. But it's really fear.

෨

*W*hen you cry, God cries with you. But He can't wipe your tears unless you let Him.

ᥫᩬ

There's better love for you. I don't know where, and I don't know when. But the only love worth having, you won't have to lie for, or steal, or hide in a box and visit on weekends.

❦

*W*hen two people are on a journey, there will be miles when they will fall silent, but that doesn't mean they shouldn't be traveling together.

৪৩

*P*atience is a virtue. Virtue is a grace. Put them all together and they make a happy face.

❧

*S*nobs aren't born; they're created.

Who you are is not your name or your family. Who you are is more essential than that; it comes from God. And what you make of yourself, that is what you give back to God.

ᏬᎧ

If you hide a lie long enough, you start to think it's the truth. But it's not. It's just a lie that lasted.

*F*unny, isn't it, how you have to be silent sometimes before you can communicate. Be still and know that He is God.

$\mathcal{P}$eople have been painting pictures and writing songs and making movies about heaven and all ever since they could breathe, but they never come close.

*S*he and Johann Bach got a lot in common. Give them a glimpse of heaven and they're off and singing. But some people, you can put heaven right smack in front of 'em, and they still can't see anything to sing about.

❧

When I get angry, I ask God for patience.

You've already been through the darkest place you can imagine. It's time to start looking for stars.

❧

*T*here are no tricks to this trade, honey. Caring, hard work, and more caring, that's what you're here for.

Remember, my darling, pride goeth before the fall.

❧

*B*aby, the only way to share his pain is to share his pain.

You took the easy way out. The same easy way out everybody else takes: You found yourself an excuse not to get involved.

‍❧

*G*od can always hear you.

*H*as God ever forsaken you? He told you He wouldn't, and He never has. Never.

Just because you feel invisible doesn't mean you are. Never give up, baby.

*S*hame brings you down. But true humility will only lift you higher.

*G*od loves you. He will walk with you all the way, but it's up to you to take the first step.

$\mathcal{E}$vil thrives when good men do nothing.

☙

*E*vil is powerful enough to make you fight back on its terms. To disarm you with your own hate. Never give in to it.

*F*ear is never harmless. It destroys from the inside.

*D*on't give up now. If God has brought you this far, He won't leave you. Will you try? Will you give Him a chance to take the fear away?

❧

*F*ather, forgive me. I forgot my faith in You. I forgot Your faith in man. I forgot who I am.

ॐ

"*V*engeance is mine, saith the Lord." I double-checked and it doesn't say, "Vengeance is mine and Tess's."

೮১

gave in to anger, and all of a sudden I saw him as he really was. The devil in a cheap suit. You'd think after all these centuries I'd get better at recognizing him.

ᑫᓗ

*B*efore you face the devil, you've got to get rid of your hate. Because his is a lot stronger than yours.

It's so easy to go from love to hate. But from hate back to love, that's the hard part.

෨

*I*f you can't find the love, let
God love through you.

You must be strong now. You must never give up. And when people make you cry, baby, and you're afraid of the dark, don't forget the light is always there.

I thought he'd be much more . . . scary, you know? Fire and brimstone. Horns.

❧

$\mathcal{F}$ree will is a gift. Love is a choice. Hate leaves you no choice at all.

*N*o generation understands the following generation's music.

*N*ever say "never" in this business. Sometimes the things you think'll never happen, do.

એ

*B*ad things are always going to happen in life. People will hurt you. But you can't use that as an excuse to fail or to hurt someone back. You only hurt yourself.

❧

I think the day comes when every daughter realizes that her mother is more than her mother, that she's another woman with a heart that can be broken, too.

*I*t's quite a world out there: disposable careers, disposable wives, disposable faith. But God's not gonna let you throw away the gift He's given you.

*T*here will be another job, but you will never have another family. Someday you're going to be lying on your deathbed and you aren't going to be saying, "Gosh, I wish I'd spent more time at the office."

❦

A little bit of hate can attract enough evil to destroy a man and everyone else he loves.

❧

It's hard to forget a friend. But it's dangerous to forget an enemy.

*Y*ou've got the most powerful weapon of all. Stick to it. Evil can't stay around when love gets there. Just be sure you are there when the moment of truth comes.

*W*herever you go, God is already there.

༄

You are who God made you,
not who your father made you.

*F*orgiveness may not change him.
It will change you.

*T*he laws of probability never seem to matter when something's happening to you.

Chance disappears when you make
a decision.

*H*ow can you judge something fairly when you don't know what the rules are? You can't play God, because you *aren't* God.

☙

*T*hat is your own life you're holding in your hands. And you can't save it any more than you can save or take someone else's life. There is only one Physician in this room today who can do that. He gave you the talent to save lives, but only He has the right to take a life or give one back. Let Him give yours back to you. Let Him help you find mercy for those who fail.

*T*hey invent clocks, and then they become slaves to them. They make up little jobs, and then they become prisoners of them. They build all sorts of roads going nowhere, and they spend all their time going up and down and back and forth.

*M*ost driven people make the mistake of thinking they're doing the driving. That's how accidents happen.

෴

You have the right to be less than perfect.

You've pushed away everyone you love just to protect a secret that you hate.

There's only one thing in this world that is truly bulletproof. It's faith. Not faith in a gun that will shoot or a radio that works or even faith in your cop's instinct. It's the faith you wrap yourself up in every day of your life. Faith that no matter what happens, you won't lose God's love. And all the bullets in the world can't pierce it. And all the pills in the world can't replace it.

*G*od loves you. And if God is on your side, what is there to fear? Nothing. Now or ever.

&

*S*ometimes it's the simplest things
that are the hardest to say . . . like,
"I'm sorry," like, "I didn't mean to
hurt you," like, "I love you," like,
"We'll get through this . . ."

❦

$\mathcal{Y}$ou keep looking at things with your eyes instead of your heart, and you'll be assuming yourself all the way back to the choir, angel girl.

❧

*S*top worrying about the problem
and start looking for the reason.

Just 'cause you don't like the horse, that's no excuse to go changing ponies midstream.

You're a man on the wrong road, and through an unusual series of events, the opportunity has come for you to make amends. And I have it on good authority that this opportunity is not coming again. May I suggest you take it by closing your mouth and opening your ears?

*T*here are great mysteries in this world that only God understands. But this I *do* understand. No mistake you may have ever made is bigger than God's power to fix it.

*R*oses are red,
Angels are gossamer.
Hold on to your souls,
And make sure you floss some
    more.
Edsels are old,
And Packards Jurassic.
But never lose faith,
'Cause your Caddy's a classic!

*W*hat have I told you about free will? This isn't some fairy tale! You don't go around flapping your wings and scaring people into living happily ever after!

❧

*F*amines, wars, and plagues have wiped out whole civilizations, but love . . . love has never been wiped out.

*T*his isn't a matter of life and death. This is a matter of life *or* death. There is a time to live and a time to die. And this is your time to live.

All you can see now is death
behind you and death ahead of
you. Stop listening to fear. Open
up those ears of yours and listen to
the Poet.

Nothing's more dangerous than loving Unless it's not loving. Look, He's not promising that it's going to be easy, but He says it's going to be worth it.

❧

*P*eople get very strange when it comes to money. I'll never understand why they put so much faith in a piece of paper.

*T*he Lord does move in
mysterious ways.

*H*ate's caused a lot of problems in this world, and it's never solved one yet.

*T*here are rivers for you to cross, but when you walk through the waters, He will be with you. There are mountains for you to climb. But when you cannot take another step . . . He will carry you. There are gardens, jungles, oceans, and caves. There are people to cherish and hearts to change. There is a life to live here. And He will hold your hand all the way if you will just come into the light and have faith.

ᕲ

*I*f it was easy, anybody could do it.

You ever notice something about humans? You ask them, if they could go back and live any day over again, what would they do? It's always to go back and fix something, as if they knew precisely the moment when everything went wrong.

ॐ

*P*eople like to think that bad things only happen to faceless strangers in newspapers, until it happens to them. That's why our faith must be strong now, *before* we need it.

❧

There's always a moment that you know, as sure as the sun, is the moment that changed your life.

ဃ

Sometimes things can seem random, because God allows us to have choices. And humans and angels can make bad ones.

❦

God can use you right now,
where you are, if you will let Him.

ော

*S*ome roads home are shorter than others. You mustn't worry about who you are leaving behind.

You know how they say love is blind? Well, sometimes it's stupid, too.

*Y*ou'd be surprised how much baggage people carry around with them. Especially the kind you can't see. Half the time it's filled with the past. And looking inside can be the most frightening and important thing a person ever does.

℃℈

*L*ove is like air. There's plenty
to go around for everybody.

*H*uman beings have the power of choice, and some of the worst choices are made in darkness.

*G*od never created anything stronger than the power of real love. It lives forever, and you never know where it's coming from next.

 споко

You can welcome death with respect and wonder, or fight it with fear and regret. Dying with regret, I've learned, is the worst of all.

*E*very prayer gets answered. Sometimes the answer is "no." But sometimes the answer is "not yet."

&

That's the problem with secrets, my friend: If you let somebody into your heart, they're gonna see what's in there.

*G*od is not the author of
confusion. He likes to write happy
endings.

*T*he first day one believes can be the most beautiful. And the most difficult. But that leap of faith is worth it.

ભ

A miracle is a fragile thing. If you don't take care of it, you can let all the truth get twisted right out of it.

∽

*A*nything from God can be
dangerous in the wrong hands.

*W*here there's an opportunity, there's an opportunist. And nothing brings 'em out of the woodwork like a good old-fashioned miracle.

*G*od loves you. He took away your disbelief. If you walk away from Him now, you do so knowing exactly Who you're turning your back on. And if a man walks away from God, where else is there to go?

လ္စာ

*G*od doesn't care how smart you are. He cares about what's in your heart.

ෆ

*G*rief is a powerful thing. It's a good thing, a healing thing. It's a way to let go of a lot of pain. But it's something to go through, not hold on to.

ৎ৵

In a family, when one person's in trouble, everyone's in trouble.

*N*othing wrong with keeping
Free Will warm while you're
waiting for it to kick in.

*G*od is not dead. He doesn't die just because you say so in a song. But a part of you dies every time you tell yourself that.

❧

You can't worship something
that's not greater than yourself.

You're all crying inside, crying alone, when what you really need is to cry together.

❧

There's something about singing the blues . . . I never heard anybody sing the yellows or the greens.

ૡ

*T*imes change. Humans call it progress. And sometimes progress is progress, but mostly it's just an excuse to tear something down.

உ

*T*hree-dimensional living is so limiting.

*H*ang in there. There's hard times ahead. War, money troubles, something called disco. But you're gonna get through it. And He'll be with you all the way.

಄

I have a message for you. You were obedient. God gave you a job to do. And now God says to you, "Well done, good and faithful servant."

Every day is a chance to start over, my friend.

இ

With God, all things are possible. I've met a lot of men who don't believe in angels, but I never met a man who didn't *want* to.

ප

*W*hy is it, if you talk to God, you're praying, but if God talks back to you, you're nuts?

*S*ometimes things get set in motion that must be played out. I'm learning that myself. God's timing is not our timing.

❧

Maybe I made a mistake, but God is using it to make something wonderful out of this. Maybe I came here by mistake, but now He's given me a new purpose.

❧

*T*here is no greater love than to give your life for your friend.

You've forgotten who God is. Nothing—not death or life or war, not the past, the present, or the future—no one, no creature on this earth, can separate you from the love of God.

❦

*G*od loves you. And He knows the secrets of your heart. The horrors that you've endured, you cannot blame Him for. You've let the past come between you and God. Turn the past over to Him. He is strong enough to take it. Give Him your future, too. And He'll make *you* strong enough to face it.

*F*unny how it always works out sooner or later, huh?

☙

*Y*ou don't need proof. You need faith.

If there's anything we should know it's how delicate life is. How little things cause big things.

*B*aby, the Doctor is in. He is *always* in.

*L*ook, I'll spell it out for you: We mess up sometimes. You haven't exactly thrown Him for a loop, you know. He can handle it. So, get over it.

❧

*O*h, excuse me. If God is willing to forgive you, who are you not to forgive yourself? You think you know better than God?

*G*od's got a plan. It's like the wind; just because you can't see it doesn't mean it's not there.

☙

*G*od loves all of His creations. And that includes you, and that includes me. God doesn't leave us when we mess up. That's when we need Him most, and He'd never leave us when we need Him.

❧

*S*ometimes the help we need is not the help we want. Do you know why God put people's faces on the front of their bodies? . . . Faces are in the front so people can see where they're going, not where they've been. We have to go forward, not backward.

The truth will hurt, but it's nothing to fear.

☙

*G*od isn't taking something away from you. God is giving you something. It's a gift. The chance to start over. God is there to mend your heart and heal your soul and break this terrible tradition of abuse. But you have to let Him in.

You can't change who you were.
But you can change who you are.
And today, you start over. Right
now. Hand it over to God. Leave it
all right here and walk away.

೮౦

*T*rying to make sense of evil will only give you a headache. Evil is for evil's sake, period. Its only goal is chaos and destruction.

ల

*T*he miracle is that there isn't more evil in this world than there is.

You know, "if" is the saddest word in the history of language . . . You hold on to that "if" long enough, it can eat a hole right into your heart.

ഐ

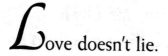 Love doesn't lie.

*G*od loves you, and His love is what gives you the strength to go on to face your failures *and* your successes.

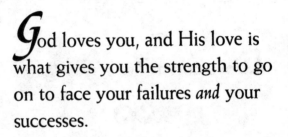

You fail because you are human.

*G*od never abandons His children. One way or the other, He triumphs every time. It's just that humans think they always have to be there to see it.

∾

*T*hings happen in God's time, not yours.

*N*ever lose hope. There is always a battle going on that you don't see.

*B*ack in the old days, communication wasn't so easy. Folks would wait weeks, months, to hear from a loved one. So they took time to write from their hearts. But nowadays it's mostly bills, sweepstakes, free detergent in little, itty-bitty boxes. Nobody's communicating anymore, they're just wasting trees.

ᏻᏻ

*N*either rain nor sleet nor snow shall keep an angel from her appointed assignment.

∾

Judging a man is easy.
Compassion is hard. You remember
that.

*H*ave you ever noticed how even people who don't believe in God find themselves calling out His name in their lowest, loneliest hour? You can't ask for His help unless somewhere, deep down, you truly believe in Him.

✌

*W*ithout faith, a man's hope is in nothing but himself. And sooner or later, he will let himself down. But God will never let us down.

Lots of people believe in God. But trusting Him . . . that is the next step.

*G*od gives purpose to everyone, but humans can still choose to hate, to kill, to destroy their lives and yours.

෨

*N*ever forget, when you have lost your faith, when God is no longer real to you—go back. Go back to the last place you saw Him. He will be waiting for you there.

Ↄↄ

Pentimento is when one painting is painted right over another. It means the artist started painting, oh, maybe a sunny day, but something changed and she painted something else right on top of it . . . People do that all the time whether they're artists or not. When they don't like something about themselves, they paint over it so no one else can see it . . . Our job is to help them expose their true colors to the light.

God has many names, you know. Jehovah, Almighty, Everlasting Father, Alpha and Omega . . . But do you know what He calls Himself? "I Am." Ask God who He is, and that is what He'll tell you. "I Am." Not "I was" or "I'm going to be." But "I am." "I am here for you now because that's where you need Me." And if God is here, right here, right now, what is there to fear?

❧

*G*od loves you. Yes, you made a mistake a long time ago. That's true . . . But somebody else took the truth and twisted it into shame. Your parents, your teachers, your friends. They made you believe their lies. You accepted their shame instead of God's love.

❧

*I*t's time for forgiveness. Forgive. Be forgiven. And God will fill you with a peace beyond all understanding.

ↅ

*D*ueling is not how people work things out these days, you know. Why don't you talk to your adversary? You could start with the truth, always a good technique. It may not be pretty, but there's a pressure cooker building up in you, and truth is kinda like a safety valve. Let it out slow and even, and maybe you won't blow up all at once.

❧

*A*ll the world is *not* a stage, and all the men and women are *not* merely players. Who you are and what you do matters to God. But how charming you are or how many autographs you sign or how many little gold statues you have on your coffee table is not going to impress the Creator of the universe. You can play all the roles you want, but it doesn't make a lick of difference if you're not playing the *one* part God wrote for you: you. Just *you*.

ॐ

"The quality of mercy is not strained . . ." Before Shakespeare said it, God *was* it. Mercy is His gift. You shine with His divine light every time you are merciful and forgive someone.

ॐ

*G*od wants you to understand that you cannot judge your parents, but you can always forgive them.

ೕ

You've never seen your father as a man, have you? Only as a hero to be worshiped. No one on this earth should be worshiped.

⌘

*G*od wants every person to be a whole person. A completely unique individual, not half of someone else.

She's not angry because she gained weight, baby. She gained weight because she's angry. At somebody, or something, or some *time* she can't forget.

ℰℐ

*G*od sees you just exactly as you are. He sees you more perfectly and more truly than people can. And He loves you more than you can ever imagine.

૯૭

We angels don't make everything okay. We just introduce you to the One Who can.

ↁ

The truth will set you free. The truth will set everybody free. But that doesn't mean it's gonna fall right into your lap. You gotta go find it first.

༄

*I*n this world there are two kinds of judgment: man's judgment and God's judgment . . . Whether someone is found guilty or acquitted, man's judgment has spoken. And whether you like the verdict or not, it is what it is. The only judgment still to be made is God's . . . I can assure you God's judgment will be more just than anything man can imagine.

*I*t's time to turn judgment into compassion. Pain into healing. Hate into forgiveness. Because when you forgive someone, you release yourself as well.

*A*nyone can give up; it's the easiest thing in the world to do. But to hold it together when everyone would understand if you fell apart, that's true strength.

*A*ll the evidence in the world can still bring a person to the wrong conclusion. But there is evidence not of this world, the evidence of things unseen that can only be seen by God.

ॐ

*H*ate is more toxic than any chemical. It poisons from the inside out. And it's a fast-acting poison; before you know it you're filled with it, and the hate is in charge. You can't control it anymore.

❧

*F*orgiveness is not a sign of
weakness, it's a sign of strength.

*H*ating is easy. Forgiveness is hard.

A lot of people think it's the imperfections that make something beautiful.

ೞ

One of the biggest mistakes we can make is to start grieving over things that haven't even happened yet.

∽

I'm not asking you to change your mind. Just bend your heart a little. Your mind will follow.

ॐ

*F*rightened people often hide behind anger.

*A*ngels don't tell you what you should have done. We're here to tell you that God loves you. He wants to deal with what you can do right now. Because "now" is all you can change.

❧

*I*sn't it odd that people pray every day over the tiniest things— the weather, a green light, a baseball game, things they can't change at all? But how come nobody prays when they are faced with a decision? When there's a difficult choice to make, don't you think God would like to help you make it?

∽

*T*imes change, people change, interest rates change, even the land itself can change. But some things, baby, they never change.

❧

You oughta pray more often. You can pray some really good ones when you get around to it. The one in the cemetery was particularly effective. And He liked the one when you were sixteen, too. What did you think, they just float up, up, and away like balloons? God's keeping track of you.

ॐ

*Y*ou've got a good heart. But every once in a while you put your faith in all the wrong things. You asked Him the other day what to do now. Well, now you know. He's put it right there in your heart, and only being afraid is going to take it out of there.

❧

*T*here's always a way out of the prisons people find themselves in, baby.

We have to fight oppression—
not with our fists, but with the
power of God.

ᏋᏋ

A coincidence is when God chooses to remain anonymous.

Your body may be in prison,
but your soul doesn't have to be.

*G*od may move in mysterious ways, baby. But people . . . their ways are the biggest mystery of all. We can't change their past, but the good news is, they can change where they're going.

☙

*H*ave you noticed something about these humans, Andrew? When life is easy, they love everyone, and everything is beautiful, and God is good. But when a human's heart gets broken, beauty suddenly disappears. The laughter of a child only brings pain, and the faith of a child is just a fire to be put out.

❧

*I*t's time to start imagining how much He loves you.

You've been looking for reasons instead of peace. And there will never be enough reasons to accept the death of your child. But God will always give you enough peace to live with it.

ಲ

You're not always going to hear the angels. When little children get older, other voices drown the angel voices out. But you should never stop listening for them. Sometimes you'll hear them in the trees. Sometimes you'll hear them in the crickets at dusk. Sometimes you'll only hear an angel in the sound of "hello." But never stop listening. And never forget that you did once hear them. And someday, you'll hear them again.

&

*W*e all have gifts, Monica. Your gift is not music, like Tess's. You don't have the gift of eternity that Andrew can bring. You have the gift of *truth*. When you speak it, people hear it. And that is cause for great joy, Monica.

❧

*G*od said there would be days like this. Days when humans behave so badly to one another that it's all an angel can do to keep loving them. The good news is, that's all you have to do.

❤

I just want you to know there's nothing to be afraid of. On one side, there is life. And on the other . . . there is life, too.

*D*o you see now how God can take the biggest mess and turn it into some good?

☙

*D*id you know that the highest form of respect for the Navajo is to call someone "Grandfather"? In fact, that's how they address God.

ᏇᎧ

*N*o, you haven't failed. Not in the sight of God. You've been a good and faithful man. You raised your children and grandchildren as the proverb says: "Train up a child in the way he should go, and when he is old, he will not depart from it." God said it, and it will happen. Whether you're there to see it or not.

❧

*T*he peace your grandfather wanted for you was not peace with *him*, but with *God*. It is not faith *in* your fathers that survives from generation to generation. It is the faith *of* your fathers. It lives here, now, and it is yours to grasp. It is the real help in times of trouble. It is the gift God has given you. Where there is faith, it is never too late.

 споро

*D*o you know what it means in English—Kaddish? It's a prayer that praises God by saying that God is above all praise. It's a prayer for the living. A gift of peace. To help you carry on.

❧

A real fisherman doesn't need to catch a thing. The joy is in the beauty of fishing. But to some people, it's all about winning.

ॐ

*G*od creates us all in His image.
There are no second-class citizens,
no minorities, no human being
greater or lesser than any other.
We are all the same in His eyes.

Good works do not necessarily make a good man. And good angels know that.

❧

*I*t's easy to love the sun when it's shining. But when it slips behind a cloud, that's when you have to brace yourself for nasty weather.

❧

*T*he problem with making heroes out of humans is that when they eventually *act* like humans, everyone is disappointed.

❧

*W*hen we ignore the truth, we ignore God, because God *is* truth. And what isn't true, He doesn't want any part of. He can't. It's just not who He is.

❧

I hate Halloween. It gives death such a bad reputation.

❧

*W*here is God? He's right here.
Where He's always been!

*H*ow come you have the power to imagine there are Martians when you don't have the power to imagine there's a God Who really exists? A God Who loves you. A God Who's never forsaken you.

&

*H*ah! Moses was patient. Job was patient. You? Not patient.

You're supposed to be a heavenly being, not a holy terror.

*G*od has a plan. He always does, but sometimes people forget and try to make their own, imperfect plans. People can only see a little way down the road. But He can see the whole trip.

ᘓᕝ

*G*od's not just a matchmaker, baby. He's a match keeper.

*L*ove may bring people together, but love doesn't always keep them together.

*H*ow can two people be married in the sight of God if they haven't asked Him to the wedding? All this work all the flowers all the invitations whats it all for without You right in the middle of it? So Lord, bless this day. Bless the couple about to marry. And bless their love and their years together.

ೲ

You must never be afraid to ask for what is good and right. You just have to know where to go to ask for it

Marriage is important. Most people never even know just how important it is. A happy marriage is a gift from God.

☙

*A*nybody can have a wedding. It takes so much more to have a marriage. That's what God wants you to have.

❧

*W*hen two people choose to become one, you become something even greater than that if you ask God into the circle, "for better, for worse, for richer, for poorer." Because when times are better, God blesses you, and when times are worse, God will bless you even more

❧

You're afraid. You're afraid that if you commit your heart and your love to someone, you'll get hurt. Well, you will. Both of you. You are going to have problems and pain and anger. You'll also have joy. Great joy.

*E*ven if every one of your good deeds was a step to heaven, it would never reach high enough. Good deeds are the evidence of your faith. But they're not a ticket to paradise.

છ

*H*ell is separation from God. It's an eternity without light. If you were on your way there, God wasn't sending you. You were sending yourself.

∽

*P*eople are always trying to build a stairway to heaven. Some are like towers, some are only a few steps high. But there's never been one that was high enough to make it all the way to God. That's when a soul has to stand on the top step and call up and say, "Here! Here I am. Please lift me up the rest of the way!" And God hears you. He reaches down and takes you home.

ᘓᘔ

*W*hen you stand before God, don't you want to see the face of a friend, instead of a stranger?

☙

I love you, God loves you, and it's just breakin' His heart to see you in this low-rent motel. You're one of His children, baby. You belong in a mansion.

❦

You've had setbacks, and you'll have others. It's not important how many times you've fallen. It's how many times you let God pick you up that matters.

❧

*G*od is faithful. He will stick with you even when you won't. He will forgive you even when you can't. His mercies are brand new every morning. This morning, He wants to give this day to you, and all the rest of your days, too. All you have to do . . . is say "yes."

*W*hy is it no one pays attention to the light until it's covered by darkness?

C∂

*T*here is mercy for you in heaven, even though it's hard to find on earth.

*S*ome people think that the word "news" comes from N-E-W-S, North, East, West, and South. It's not true, but it made me think. That's where the news comes from —all the four corners of the world. But where does the truth come from? Someplace else entirely. I come from that place where truth lives. I'm an angel.

&

*G*od loves you. He wants you to be His child, not His avenger. You find the facts, but let Him reveal the truth. Because He's the only one who knows it. All of it.

❧

*G*od is not the source of confusion. He is the source and completer of your faith. And that is what you need now. Faith that God knows who you really are. Yes, you are not perfect. *No one* is perfect. *No one*. But God's love is perfect. And no one can love us better than He can.

❧

*N*othing made by God is queer.
God loves all his creations.

*E*very person on this earth is like a violin. Whatever wood we're made of, whatever unique and distinctive qualities we have, the music is always the purest and the most beautiful when we put ourselves in the hands of the Master.

*N*othing meaningful ever really gets forgotten. It can always be found by those willing to look.

*S*ometimes when the people who love us hurt us, the only way to find out why is to ask questions. Maybe you need to look deeper.

Every parent makes mistakes. The only one who hasn't is God. He gave the right daughter to the right mother. The best way to thank Him is to honor her.

You see, with God, there is no time. Yesterday, today, and tomorrow all belong to Him, right now. And He's willing to give it all to you this instant, if you'll accept it.

❧

Some people think they need a lot of things they don't really need.

*F*unny thing, isn't it? How people who think holding something pretty over their heads is gonna keep 'em safe and dry. Then it rains. And they realize they've been putting their faith in a little, itty-bitty piece of paper that's gonna fall apart when they need it the most.

❧

I bet you started smoking 'cause you wanted to feel like you "belonged." Let me ask you something: How many more do you have to light up before it starts to work?

༄

*D*on't go questioning what the Lord has planned for you. You may be in the car, but He's holding the map!

෩

*G*od has a message for you, baby.
He wants you to know that He
loves you that only He can fill that
emptiness inside. You just gotta let
His truth in.

ஐ

You have your eyes on the wrong prize. Whatever you think you've gotta win, He's already won for you, if you'll just take hold of it. The real prize is God and His love. Set your eyes on that, honey. That's the only thing worth winning.

*G*od wants you to fall to your knees and take your future back while you still have the chance.

You've got to stop looking at yourself through your eyes and see yourself through God's eyes.

You have always belonged.
You've always been a child of God,
and that should have been enough.
But you want more. And at what
price? What is it going to matter if
you gain the whole world and lose
your soul? Hmmmm?

ᑯ

❧

About
Martha Williamson

As executive producer and head writer of the hit CBS drama *Touched By An Angel* and the popular new series *Promised Land*, Martha Williamson is the first woman to solely executive produce two hour-long dramas simultaneously on network television.

Williamson began writing for television in 1984. Her work has been honored with such awards as the Templeton Prize, the Anti-Defamation League's Deborah Award, the Catholics in Media Associates Award, the Covenant Award, the Excellence in Media

Award, the Gabriel Award, the Swiss American Faith and Values Award, the Edward R. Murrow Responsibility in Television Award, the 1997 Christopher Award, and the prestigious Producer's Guild Nova Award.

A native of Denver, Colorado, Williamson received her Bachelor of Arts degree from Williams College. She currently resides in Los Angeles.